SHARKS

WHALE SHARKS

JOHN F. PREVOST

ABDO & Daughters

Published by Abdo & Daughters, 4940 Viking Drive, Suite 622, Edina, Minnesota 55435.

Library bound edition distributed by Rockbottom Books, Pentagon Tower, P.O. Box 36036, Minneapolis, Minnesota 55435.

Printed in the United States.

Cover Photo credit: Peter Arnold, Inc.
Interior Photo credits: Peter Arnold, Inc.

Edited by Bob Italia

Library of Congress Cataloging-in-Publication Data

Prevost, John F.
   Whale sharks / John F. Prevost.
      p. cm. — (Sharks)
   Includes bibliographical references (p. 23) and index.
   ISBN 1-56239-473-8
1. Whale shark—Juvenile literature. [1. Whale shark. 2. Sharks.] I. Title.
II. Series: Prevost, John F. Sharks.
QL638.95.R4P74 1995
597'.31—dc20   95-6375
                                                             CIP
                                                             AC

ABOUT THE AUTHOR
   John Prevost is a marine biologist and diver who has been active in conservation and education issues for the past 18 years. Currently he is living inland and remains actively involved in freshwater and marine husbandry, conservation and education projects.

Contents

WHALE SHARKS AND FAMILY

Sharks are fish without **scales**. A rough covering of **denticles** protects their skin. Sharks do not have bones. Their skeleton is made of **cartilage**, a tough, stretchy tissue.

Whale sharks are the world's largest fish. They are slow-moving giants that strain food in their **gills**. Nurse sharks and sand sharks are closely related to the whale shark.

Whale sharks are the world's largest fish.

WHAT THEY LOOK LIKE

Whale sharks are giant fish. The largest recorded whale shark was 45 feet (13.7 meters) long. Most are 13 to 39 feet (4 to 12 meters) long.

Whale sharks have wide, flattened heads. They are thick-bodied sharks that swim near the water surface. Their backs are marked with light spots and stripes that form a checkerboard pattern.

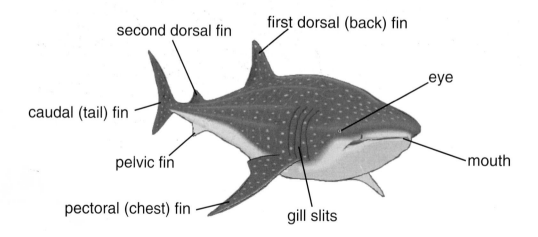

second dorsal fin

first dorsal (back) fin

eye

caudal (tail) fin

pelvic fin

mouth

pectoral (chest) fin

gill slits

Most sharks share the same features.

Whale sharks have wide, flattened heads. They are thick-bodied sharks that swim near the water surface.

Whale sharks may be found alone or in **schools** of over 100 members.

WHERE THEY LIVE

Whale sharks may travel along a coast or swim far out in the ocean. These sharks like **temperate** water, 70° to 77° F (21° to 25° C). They follow the **seasonal** changes in water temperatures. **Schools** of tuna and **mackerel** are often found nearby.

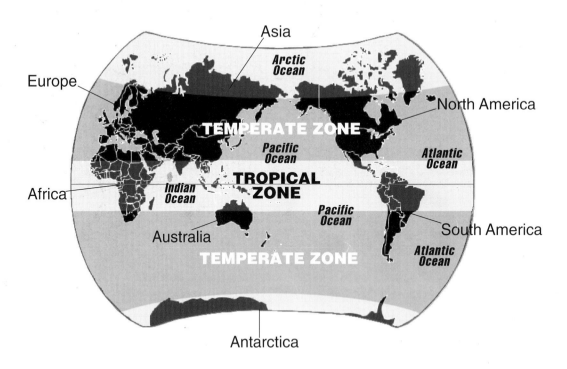

Whale sharks prefer warm water. This shark is swimming near the Ningaldo Reef, Australia.

FOOD

All sharks are **predators**. They eat other animals. The whale shark feeds near the surface, with its tail down and head up. It sucks water into its huge mouth, trapping its **prey**. The water is forced out through the shark's **gills** and the trapped prey is swallowed.

Whale sharks eat **sardines**, small **mackerel**, tuna, **squid**, and small shellfish. Floating plants are also eaten.

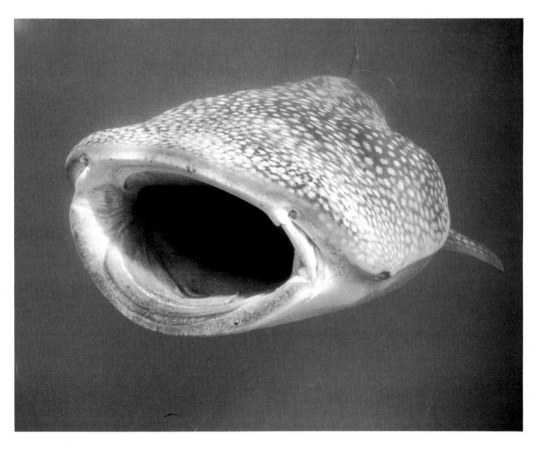

The whale shark sucks water into its huge mouth when feeding.

SENSES

Because they are so large, whale sharks must find plenty of food. The senses of smell and taste are well developed. Sense **organs** are located all over their body.

Because eyesight is not important to the whale shark, its eyes are small. Whale sharks can sense **electric fields**. They share this skill with other sharks. All animals with nervous systems give off a weak electric field. The whale shark's skill to sense electric fields helps it find **prey** it cannot see.

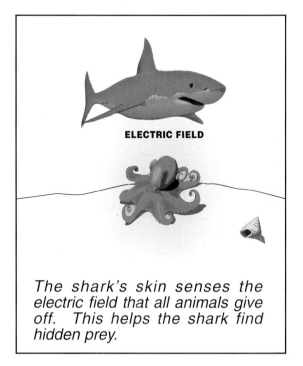

ELECTRIC FIELD

The shark's skin senses the electric field that all animals give off. This helps the shark find hidden prey.

Because eyesight is not important to the whale shark, its eyes are small.

BABIES

Newborn whale sharks are called pups. The smallest pups are 21 to 22 inches (53 to 56 cm) long. The young hatch from eggs inside their mother and are born live. Some females have up to 16 egg cases in them, but **litter** size is not known. The pups are on their own once they are born.

Young whale sharks hatch from eggs inside their mother and are born live.

ATTACK AND DEFENSE

The whale shark's large mouth is not made to grab large **prey**. Though its teeth are tiny, there are over 300 rows per jaw. Its only **predator** might be an adult great white shark. Large sharks and killer whales will eat smaller whale sharks.

The whale shark's only defense is its thick skin. It protects the shark from predators that do not have cutting teeth. The thick skin also makes the whale shark less appealing to other predators.

The whale shark's mouth is not made to grab prey. Its only real defense against predators is its thick skin.

ATTACKS ON HUMANS

Whale sharks are little threat to humans. Sometimes divers approach and ride these large sharks. But their huge tail can injure a diver. Whale sharks have bumped into boats. Often it is the boaters who run into these giant fish.

Divers often approach whale sharks. But they must be careful around the whale shark's tail, which is very large and powerful.

WHALE SHARK FACTS

Scientific Name:

Whale shark: *Rhiniodon typus*

Synonyms, or other scientific names for *R. typus:*
Rhincodon typus, Rhineodon typus, Rhinodon typus.

Average Size: 39 feet (12 meters) long

45 feet (13.7 meters) long—
largest measured

Where They're Found: All over the world in **tropical**
and **temperate** seas.

The whale shark.

GLOSSARY

Cartilage (CAR-till-ej): A tough, stretchy tissue forming parts of an animal's skin.

Denticle (DEN-ti-kul): A small tooth-like structure that protects a shark's skin and makes it rough to the touch.

Electric field: The electric-charged area surrounding an animal's body, created by the nervous system.

Gills: The part of a fish by which the animal gets oxygen from water.

Litter: The young animals born at one time.

Mackerel: A food and game fish related to the tuna, having a silvery body.

Organ: A part of an animal or plant that is made up of several kinds of tissue and performs a specific function, like the heart or eyes.

Pelvic fin: A fin found at the lower part of a fish's body.

Predator (PRED-uh-tor): An animal that hunts and eats other animals.

Prey: An animal that is hunted for food.

Sardine: A food fish that is related to the herring.

Scales: Platelike structures forming all or part of the outer covering of certain animals, such as snakes and fish.

School: A large group of fish or water animals of the same kind swimming together.

Seasonal: Something that happens with the seasons.

Species: A group of related living things that shares basic characteristics.

Squid: A group of sea animals related to the octopus that is streamlined and has at least ten arms.

Temperate (TEM-prit): Moderate to cool water located between the polar and tropical waters.

Tropical (TRAH-pih-kull): The part of the Earth near the equator where the oceans are very warm.

BIBLIOGRAPHY

Budker, Paul. *The Life of Sharks.* London: Weidenfeld and Nicolson, 1971.

Compagno, Leonard. FAO Species Catalogue Vol. 4, *Sharks of the World.* United Nations Development Programme, Rome, 1984.

Gilbert, P. W., ed. *Sharks, Skates, and Rays.* Maryland: Johns Hopkins Press, 1967.

Macquitty, Miranda. *Shark.* New York: Alfred A. Knopf, 1992.

Sattler, Helen. *Sharks, the Super Fish.* New York: Lothrop, Lee & Shepard Books, 1986.

Server, Lee. *Sharks.* New York City: Gallery Books, 1990.

Index